UNMOORED

Women Translating Women
A collaborative project of the Ashoka Centre for Translation, the Susham Bedi Memorial Fund and Zubaan Publishers

The Ashoka Centre for Translation, through its initiatives, is committed to thinking about translation from a many-to-many perspective to foster India's multilingual ethos. The Women Translating Women project, under which this book has been supported, is a joint initiative of the Centre and the Susham Bedi Memorial Fund. The Fund, established in memory of the Hindi poet and author Susham Bedi (1 July 1945–20 March 2020), supports the publication of 12 books over two years by Zubaan Publishers.

translation.ashoka.edu.in
sushambedi.com
zubaanbooks.com

UNMOORED

Ramachandran Usha
Translated by Krupa Ge

zubaan

ZUBAAN
128 B Shahpur Jat, 1st floor
NEW DELHI 110 049
Email: contact@zubaanbooks.com
Website: www.zubaanbooks.com

First published by Zubaan Publishers Pvt. Ltd 2024

10 9 8 7 6 5 4 3 2 1

ISBN 978 81 94253 35 8 (paperback)
ISBN 978 81 94253 37 2 (ebook)

Zubaan is an independent feminist publishing house based in New Delhi with a strong academic and general list. It was set up as an imprint of India's first feminist publishing house, Kali for Women, and carries forward Kali's tradition of publishing world quality books to high editorial and production standards. *Zubaan* means tongue, voice, language, speech in Hindustani. Zubaan publishes in the areas of the humanities, social sciences, as well as in fiction, general non-fiction, and books for children and young adults under its Young Zubaan imprint.

Typeset in Sabon 11/16.
Printed and bound at Chaman Offset.

Unmoored

1

Ameera was told she would leave prison today. She signed wherever the female Dubai prison official asked her to, scribbling her name down in Arabic, her hands trembling. Then she found a chair and sat down wordlessly. The clock on the wall across the room read five minutes to six. They had informed her yesterday that officials from the Indian embassy would come to see her at six.

Beyond the undrawn curtains the sun was beating down hard. Summer. It wouldn't grow dark till 7.30. She looked at the telephone on the table and almost instantaneously banished the thought. They certainly wouldn't allow it. *What if I get into trouble for asking to make a call, why mess it up just as I am about to leave?* She tried to resist the thought again. But she just could not stop thinking about her five-year-old, Saif.

Even as her fingers worked the tasbih beads, her mind was racing. She didn't know what the papers she'd signed said—she couldn't read. She knew just about enough Arabic to sign her own name. Was the woman official right? Was she really about to be released? Had her mercy petition been accepted? Had the Indian embassy official who'd been trying to have Ameera released been successful? She had no way of knowing. She slipped back into prayer.

When she had been sentenced, he was just a year and a half old, and in the four years she had been in prison they had let her see him just once. He might even have started school by now. Did he remember his mother? Would she ever see him again? When? Maybe one day, as a grown up, he would come looking for her. She felt her stomach churn as she thought more and more about what might happen. 'Ya Allah,' she sighed.

As she sat there weeping, unable to even wipe away her tears, eyes trained on the floor, they called out to her, those Indian faces. That salwar-kameez-wearing person with the big-bindi-on-the-forehead face, the one who'd fought hard for her release. Payal Sharma, who had come to meet Ameera countless times in prison.

'All that praying of yours was not in vain, beti. Today's your release. You're going home to Madras. Ready? Shall we leave?' Payal said in Hindi, smiling.

Ameera, still in tears, hugged her.

'Shukriya,' she finally managed to say.

Ameera got in the car and turned around to look at the prison she had been lodged in, punished for no crime of her own. She couldn't believe she was free, just as she had begun preparing to be sentenced to death. Then she grew agitated again. She wanted to see Saif one last time. Who could she ask though? She remained quiet instead.

She looked out as the vehicle moved through Dubai's busy, busy roads and reached the Indian embassy. A few people at the entrance turned around to look at her as officers rushed her into the building. Inside, another officer was ready with all her paperwork.

'Your papers and your ticket are in here. We will go straight to the airport now and will leave you after we hand you over to the officers there. They will be with you until you are seated safely inside the aircraft. Once you reach Chennai, our colleagues will receive you and do everything they can to help you. You don't have to talk to anyone about anything,' he said in Hindustani.

Ameera nodded, still speechless. Just then, another woman about Ameera's age entered the room looking utterly flustered. Her face was red, she must have cried a lot.

'Mohan Sir, is my duplicate passport ready?' she asked in Tamil, and Ameera turned and looked at her. How long it had been since she had last heard Tamil. When the officer asked the other woman not to worry in that familiar tongue, Ameera finally found her voice and asked if she could make a phone call. Tamil, an informal dialect, with hints of Urdu, from a woman who could pass as an Arab, that's how fair Ameera was, veiled in black—the entire room turned to look at her.

'My son, he's only five, my baby. Before I go back home let me see him once,' Ameera asked, her voice breaking, her eyes begging.

'The number?'

Ameera thought for a bit and finally remembered a neighbour. She gave the officer a phone number and a name. He dialled and handed the phone to her. When she said her name she got a 'wrong number' and a rude response in Arabic. Then the line was cut. She had two more numbers. Both times, just as she said her name they hung up.

Finally, the officer picked up the phone, dialled the number she had first given him, and said in a stern official-sounding tone that Ameera was out of prison, that she was going home to India that very day, and that she wanted to see her son one last time. This time the voice on the line seemed accommodating. The officer gave them a brief summary—her release from prison, her flight details—and hung up.

Ameera went and stood by the window, looking at a twinkling Dubai, its many night lights, and the cars that went up and down the road. Before she knew it, she was crying again. Then she remembered something and made another call. This time she was lucky. They heard her story, their voice tinged with sadness, and the answers from the voice on the phone gave her some confidence.

Payal walked up to Ameera and smiled, compassion in her eyes. Ameera wanted to know why they finally let her out of prison. The officer took her by her hands and led her to a quiet corner of the room to tell her about her release.

Ameera heard someone in the room say, 'The flight is at one, we should get ready to leave now if we want to make it in time.' She got up and held Payal's arms, fumbling for words that could convey just how thankful she felt. Payal wrapped her arms around Ameera's shoulders and wished her and Saif a good future.

'Eat this and go,' she said, and left some food and water on the table for Ameera.

Ameera asked to go to the bathroom. Tears and more tears as she closed the door behind her. *Once, just once, just one last time, show me my son, dear God,* she cried, slapping herself across the face over and over again. She calmed down after losing herself to tears for a few minutes. Then she wiped her face, covered it, and walked out. She ate Indian food for the first time in years. It was so satisfying that she even felt a little brave after eating it. She got in the vehicle that was to drop her at the airport and looked at the woman next to her, gathering that her name was Indumathi and that she too was going to Chennai. The other officer—Mohan Kumar—and Payal reassured the two women again. They'd get them onto the flight and make sure they reached their relatives in Chennai safely.

When she got out of the car, Indumathi tried to speak to Mohan and Payal, to thank them, but a Sudani policewoman rushed over, took all the paperwork from them, and shoved them both to get them into the airport.

Ameera wouldn't go inside yet. She pleaded with the security officer in Arabic. But before she could finish her sentence the policewoman grabbed her arm and pulled her inside.

As Ameera turned around, disappointed, Indumathi's eyes met hers. Those beautiful eyes. Indu could see no more than those eyes and the veil. And yet those eyes, they told Indu that this woman was breathtaking.

What a gorgeous woman, Indu thought to herself as she watched Ameera try to cross the security barrier and go out, chanting 'Allah!' over and over again. The Sudani policewoman's strong arms stopped Ameera, but when she pleaded again in Arabic, the policewoman gestured to her and sent her out of the airport.

2

A little boy who looked younger than five was outside, draped in a beautiful white dishdasha, complete with the headscarf.

'Saif! Saif!' Ameera cried. She picked him up and showered him with kisses.

The child, however, went stiff and tried to wriggle out of her grip as if he were meeting a stranger. The old woman who had brought Saif to Ameera tried to hand her a plastic bag, but the policewoman snatched it from her to inspect it. Ameera didn't care about any of this. Sobbing, she talked to the child non-stop. The policewoman handed the bag to Ameera and in that stern voice ordered her to stop talking, to start walking. There was nothing she could do now. Ameera handed her child back to the old woman, told her in Arabic to take good care of him, and hesitantly took one step after another behind the policewoman. But her eyes, she didn't take them off that child. When she reached the gate, she couldn't resist going back for one last hug. Still in tears, she hugged him tight and kissed his face over and over again, and then she kneeled beside Saif. 'Fi Amanillah.' She held her hands up in prayer, and asked her God to take care of her son.

People began to stare at her. Then the boy began to cry; he was scared. When the policewoman, in that strict, intimidating way, said that it was time to leave again, Ameera got up and walked away. Her eyes wet, she looked, unblinking, taking in the last sight of her son, waving goodbye, until he disappeared. Once he vanished, she fell into a chair on the side of the pathway with a loud thud. Indumathi felt helpless watching her cry quietly. The policewoman, who had seen too many of these kinds of events, seemed unbothered by what had happened and stood there just looking at the crying woman. After a few minutes, she tapped Ameera's shoulder to signal that she had to walk again. Ameera got a hold on herself and walked.

The two women followed the police officer through the sixth largest airport in the world. She accompanied them through immigration, ensured their passports were stamped, checked them in, helped seat them both, and then got off the airplane. As the plane taxied, Indumathi became restless and anxious. The air hostess saw her panicking and brought her something to drink. As the airplane got on the runway and prepared to take off, she began to sweat profusely.

'Kanda sashti kavasam,' she chanted and noticed the prayer beads in Ameera's hands. Ameera was praying too, very quietly. The peace she saw in Ameera's eyes took Indu by surprise.

The airplane wasn't full. It was just the two of them in their row. No one came to claim the third seat.

'Was that your son?' Indu asked softly, and Ameera nodded.

The plane steadied after a while. They ate the food the air hostess gave them, and then the lights went off. Everyone else seemed to be dozing off, so Indu decided to nap too.

Just three days ago she had boarded her first flight to Dubai. She hadn't known then that her dreams, all of them, would come crashing down like this. She'd go to the Nanganallur Anjaneyar Temple as soon as she was home in Chennai. *What grave danger I've escaped.* Just thinking about it made the hair on her arms stand up. *I am home safe, Shankar.* She thought of the man she had fallen in love with and married. *Poor Shankar, he must have been so scared. He needn't worry anymore.* Thinking about him brought her some calm, and she got a little more comfortable in her seat, stretching her legs.

Ten days ago, Shankar had surprised her by coming home early from work. 'Indu, remember the lady we met the day we went to see the Dubai agent, the one who runs a consultancy?' he asked.

'Srividya, right? I remember her pretty well.'

'Someone she knows runs a shopping complex in Dubai. They're looking to hire a lady accountant urgently. She called me at work today to ask if you'd be interested. If you are willing, she says she will arrange the visa. The pay is pretty good and the stay is free. Eight-hour duty.'

'I guess it's a good thing I gave her my visiting card,' Indu said, though she was a bit taken aback. For two years, her engineer husband had been looking for a job in Dubai so he could earn in dirhams. But now a job for her?

'You —' she started.

'Don't worry. She says she'll find me a job in six months. Be bold, go first. Once I get a good job you can let yours go. What do you say?' Indu had nodded in agreement.

'That lady, Srividya Madam, how smart she was. I saw her visiting card, it said she had a Master's degree from London.' Indu had also sung Srividya's praises that day.

She remembered Srividya's face from the day they first met. Cotton saree, subtle make-up, a middle-aged woman who commanded respect.

That evening Indu and Shankar met Srividya again. Indu agreed to take on the job and handed over her passport. In just a week her visa, ticket, everything she needed had been arranged. The couple didn't realise then that they had walked into a trap and had even celebrated the sudden windfall.

3

Indu was to board the flight at eleven in the morning. She wasn't sure if she would get sticker bindis in Dubai, so she asked Shankar to go buy some from the store nearby. 'Shouldn't you have planned and bought all this earlier?' he muttered under his breath as he went out, but he came back looking really happy half an hour later and called out to her.

'Do you remember Padmanabhan, who lives across from Raghavendra Swamy Mutt? His wife's relative lives in Dubai. He's given me the relative's mobile number and address,' Shankar began. 'He even called him while I was there and told him you are coming. Mohan Kumar. Works in the Indian embassy. He said you can call him if you need help. In fact, he asked if he should come to the airport to receive you. I said there's no need. Srividya Madam asked me just yesterday if we know anyone in Dubai. Anyway, I wrote his number and address down on this bindi packet. Keep it with you,' he said and placed the packet safely in the inner pocket of her handbag and zipped it up.

Neither of them knew just how important that number on the packet would turn out to be. She could never forget Padmanabhan, who was godsent, or his relative Mohan Kumar and everything he had done for her. *Raghavendra! Saviour of orphans! Friend of those in need!* She gave thanks to the saint. She got up to go to the bathroom. The thing that she had hated, that she had dismissed as an inconvenience every month until now, had also come to her rescue.

Ameera saw her get up and got up too. The two women joined the queue in front of the toilet. Indu went in, came out, and waited for Ameera. As Ameera walked out adjusting her burqa, the woman who was waiting to enter the toilet gasped in that familiar Madras Tamil, 'Ya Allah, is it Ameera?'

'Maami!' Ameera rushed to hug the other woman.

Ameera's body shook as she wept in the old lady's arms.

'Everyone's looking, wipe your tears,' the old lady said. 'I knew you'd be released. I just didn't know it was going to be today.' The old woman patted Ameera's back with tender affection. She looked at Indu and smiled sadly.

When they returned to their seats, Ameera laid her head on the old woman's lap and said, 'Ayesha Maami, I will never forget your help, I'll think of you with gratitude until I die.'

'It wasn't just me, Ameera. My elder arbab, the boss who's in London, he spoke many, many times with both the government and your family. Your husband's other wives demanded quite a lot as blood money, devil's spawns, he even bargained with them and brought the amount down to five lakh rupees. He gave them some money too. And then our embassy collected funds, that lady Payal Sharma and others, they even placed ads in newspapers and collected money. May they all be well!' Ayesha said. 'Alright, alright. That's enough. It's all taqdeer, child. People can see you now, wipe your face.'

Ameera sat up straight.

'They did all that, yes, but you started the efforts, Maami. Payal Sharma told me just how much you did.'

Ameera's veil was now off her face. Indu couldn't take her eyes off her. 'How beautiful,' she said, without realising she was saying it out loud.

'Beauty! Her beauty is the source of all her trouble,' Ayesha said. 'Are you Tamil? You're no different from her, except that you are dusky. You are beautiful yourself. You've come with Ameera, have you? Are you a policewoman?' The questions were rapid.

'No. I was in some trouble, I've just got away from it all,' Indu said.

'Were you also in jail?'

'No, no.' Indu was flustered. Jail? Was Ameera in jail? What could she have done to go to jail? She looked so harmless. She didn't look cruel enough to kill someone.

Did she run someone over with a car? She knew that blood money was given to the families of victims. If you gave them money, several lakhs, they might even forgive you and you could get out of a prison sentence; she had read that this was the law in some Islamic nations.

'Enough now, don't cry, Ameera. Too much money always leads to trouble. His other wives had him bumped off and got you arrested for it. You think they will ever live well?'

Indu couldn't hear what Ayesha said after this. They had lowered their voices and were speaking about personal matters. Indu turned away and looked out the window to give them some privacy.

After a while, Ameera wiped her face and adjusted her veil. Ayesha got up and went back to her seat.

The updates Ayesha Maami gave Ameera about her brother and the rest of her family worried her. She hadn't seen her brother, his wife, their kids, or her sisters in six years. She searched for all of their faces in her memories as she thought of them one after the other. How could this decision, which she had taken for all their sakes, so that they could all live well, have gone so wrong?

'Whom did I wrong? Why did I rot in that dark cell for three years when I did nothing? Allah?!' Her eyes closed, heavy and tired.

4

As the flight began its gentle descent to Chennai, both of them slipped into anxiety. When the doors opened, the air hostess handed the two women over to an officer waiting at the entrance of the aircraft. The women walked swiftly with the officer, and he helped them with the immigration formalities. Then they were taken into another room.

You could tell these were senior officers just by looking at them.

'You don't have to worry about anything, the Chief Minister will meet you soon and make arrangements for a job as well. You can call this number if you need anything,' one said. 'You've understood what I said?' he asked Ameera, and she nodded.

Some more signatures on papers, and then the two women were brought out. Ameera's eyes landed on her brother and sister-in-law—she ran to them and embraced them. Her brother looked older; Anni looked just the same.

'Where's the child, di?

'It's their child. They won't give him up. Their child belongs to them. That's the custom there.' Ameera choked on her words.

'Ya Allah! What cruelty is this? A child does not belong to their mother?' Anni was in utter shock, a hand on her face. 'You didn't bring anything from there?'

Her brother Yousuf intervened then, signalling to her sister-in-law to keep quiet.

'They have sent some clothes, jewels, and a draft for 10,000 rupees. I stayed in that house for just three years, even handed my child over to them. I have come back as your burden,' Ameera said.

Anni had eyes only for the bag. 'Some four pieces of clothing and ten sovereigns of gold, it looks like.' Her tone dripping with sarcasm, she had revealed her real self pretty quickly. Ameera felt fear grip her gut.

Indu walked with the officers, looking for her husband, her eyes moving from one person to another. No sign of him anywhere. She didn't know whom to call, and what would she say, anyway? Then she saw Ameera speaking with her relatives. She approached them slowly.

'Did no one come to receive you?' Ameera asked, before quickly introducing Indu to her family. Just then, Ayesha, who was pushing a trolley piled with one too many boxes, came towards them.

Another round of introductions.

'This is my son Akbar Ali. Engineer. And this is my daughter Mehrunnisa. She's a schoolteacher now. Her husband's a college professor.'

Indu gave Ayesha's son and daughter a polite smile.

Pointing at Indu, Ameera's Anni said to Ayesha, 'No one's come to take her home.'

Indu reluctantly asked for a mobile phone. Ayesha took Akbar's mobile phone and handed it over. She dialled a number and got a 'not in use' message. Was Shankar unwell? Had he been in an accident? Her head filled with ugly thoughts.

When Ayesha said, 'Call your relatives, anyone you know. Or else I will take you home, don't worry,' Indu keyed in her landlord's number.

'Maami, Indu here,' she said.

'Are you calling from Dubai? Listen, last night Shankar packed up everything and vacated the house. He didn't really tell me anything. Did he find a job in Dubai as well?'

Her landlord continued speaking but Indu couldn't process what she'd heard. 'Did he say where he was going, Maami?' she pressed.

'I don't know all that much, ma, yesterday morning a lot of his people came to see him. Your sister-in-law, I think, the one that lives in Tambaram, she also came. Shankar asked me to look at the accounts and deposit any remaining rent advance into his bank account, handed over the house keys, picked up everything in your house, and left. He didn't even look at us or speak to us properly, you know? Maama felt really bad,' the voice on the line continued. Indu's hands cut the call involuntarily.

She didn't have the strength to cry. So she just sat there. She figured out what was going on, though. Clearly, he hadn't believed her when she'd said that she'd escaped unscathed from Dubai. Was this all the love he could muster for her? Four years they'd lived together as man and wife, did he not even believe in their marriage? Just the previous evening when she'd called from the Indian embassy to tell him about her escape, he'd been a source of courage and solace.

'Just knowing you're safe is enough. Please come home to me,' he'd said then. Who had said what to him now? Had he changed his mind so soon? Did he not believe her when she said she hadn't let anything happen to her? Where should she go now? Maybe she could go see her uncle in Madurai? Would he not ask a thousand and eight questions? She'd married Shankar against everyone's wishes. She didn't really have any close friends. She had lived as if the man she loved was her world.

Questions for which she had no answers began to crowd her head; everything seemed briefly dark, fear consumed her. Without realising she needed it, she held on to Ayesha's trolley for support. Then, finally, the tears found her. Ayesha took her aside and sat her down in a chair. She held out the tiny bottle of water in her hand. Indu finished all the water in one big gulp. Ayesha held Indu by the shoulder and asked, 'What happened, ma?' Indu began to cry loudly.

'This woman told me she would employ me. She took me to Dubai and tried to throw me in the gutter there. But I ran away. I think my husband didn't believe anything I told him. Ours was a love marriage; his whole family ostracised us. My father died when I was very young, and last year I lost my mother too. I have no siblings. Where do I go now?' Indu began to hit herself on the head, still weeping, sputtering out all the information she could.

The officers who were still with her spoke among themselves for a bit. They asked Indu if she would like to stay in a home for destitute women. Ayesha stepped up. 'Sir, if she's okay with it, I'll take her home. Let her stay with us for a few days, we'll try reaching her family in the meanwhile. If nothing works out, she can think about the home.' Her son tried to stop Ayesha, but she brushed him aside. 'Listen, Akbaru, what sort of people are we if we don't help someone in need? Sir, here, you take my passport, write my address down. Make a copy of my passport if you want to.'

Indu felt that going with Ayesha was the right thing to do. It sounded much better than going to a home for destitute women. Ameera, too, felt that this was the right thing for Indu. She didn't have a choice anyway. And so, even if a bit hesitantly, Indumathi left the airport with Ayesha.

5

Behind Saidapet Magistrate Court, beyond Srinagar Colony in Rangarajapuram, Ayesha's home was abustle, ready to welcome her. The large cab Akbar Ali had arranged dropped them off in front of the house. Ayesha got out of the car. She had last come home five years ago for Mehrunnisa's wedding.

In the past, every time she had returned, her mother had waited at the entrance to welcome Ayesha with tears in her eyes. Would her umma's spirit wait at the entrance to welcome her now? She stood there taking it all in.

A tiled roof, a small porch, and behind that just one room for everything and for everyone. In that room, she had lived with her father and umma. Later, when she'd married and then separated from her husband, she'd made this her home again with her mother and two children. In this house, she'd fought off life's many difficulties. That tiny tiled home was now a sparkling bungalow which the neighbourhood looked at in awe, and her kids had been educated well. All of this was possible because of that mother of hers, was it not?

'Amma has left us all and gone,' someone in the crowd that had gathered to welcome her said, and a few people began to weep. Ayesha cut them off.

'Look, don't talk about all that, it's been over a year since her maut. Why sing dirges now, huh? Besides, my mother hasn't gone anywhere, she's right here. Listen, Senthil Amma, didn't you borrow Umma's green silk saree for your niece's wedding? Did you return it to her finally or not?'

Laughter rippled through the crowd as Ayesha lightened the mood.

Senthil's mother Maragatham tried to laugh through her tears. 'Mehr Amma, you are back at it as always with your playfulness.'

Ayesha spoke to everyone, inquiring after their well-being. Akbar Ali asked Mehrunnisa to take Indu into the house.

'See, Ma, how is the house looking? All of our relatives that have come to see it have gone back with heartburn. Our Meesapettai Aunty's son Peer Ali is studying architecture, no? I designed the house with him and whipped it into shape. There are two bedrooms down here, and two more rooms upstairs. This is all we can do on a plot this size, though. It's cost us forty lakhs so far. The house next door is going on sale. Shall we buy it?' Akbar Ali asked expectantly.

'No need, pa. The big sheikh's wife has passed away and no one there is keen on keeping me employed now that she's gone. I also want to be around my grandchildren. You know, with this diabetes and blood pressure I've decided I want to be at ease, be around our people. That's why I've come back. When you have your nikkah, we can stay downstairs; we will settle Mehr upstairs, and let's all live together, raasa.'

No one said anything then. Akbar met his older sister's eyes and Mehr asked Ayesha, 'Do you still have a work visa or has it been cancelled?'

Ayesha's face fell. She opened her mouth to say something.

Just then, Akbar interjected, 'Alright, alright, let's talk about all this later. Now you eat and get some rest.' He looked at his sister. 'Mehru, you call Nidur and let Vappa know that Umma is back.' Akbar then went out.

Call Nidur? What was this new connection between her children and their father? Had they forgotten his betrayal, how he had left behind the woman he had married, the children he had fathered, and set up another home with another woman? It looked like all the troubles she'd left behind were going to crop up again now that she was back. What new problems could come her way anyway, she wondered and laughed. She went to look for Indumathi.

Indu was seated on the bed in the comfortable room the family had given her. She wasn't in a state to think about what awaited her next. Ayesha gently opened the door, and their eyes met.

'Take your bath and come out, ma. I have asked them to make moringa sambar for you. Look at me: you are educated, you will surely get a job somehow. Be brave. Once upon a time, I too was left stranded, that too with two kids. You go to the college you studied at and ask for your certificates; I hear they'll issue them again for you. Until then, no matter how long it takes, you stay here. I have two tenants in the portion just behind this house. And there's one room that's empty now. I will have the room cleaned. You will be safe there, you wait and see.'

When Ayesha handed over four new sets of salwar kameez, Indumathi was astonished.

'I bought these for girls in my family that live here. They will fit you well, I think. Wear them. If you don't like the kind of clothes we wear—it's all silk you know—or if you don't like the colours, we can go to Saravana Stores in T Nagar later and buy something to your liking.'

'Amma!' Indu rested her head on Ayesha's shoulders.

For a few moments, Ayesha allowed her to cry in silence in her arms. Then she said, 'Look, ma, first you stop crying. What has happened for you to cry like this?

We can talk to your husband and his people too. Be brave.'

'I have no one but you in this world right now,' Indu said.

She picked up her clothes and went into the bathroom with its shiny new tiles and marble. She turned the shower on. Hot water and red-hot tears streamed down her face right away. 'Shankar, Shankar,' she gasped. Was he so cowardly, was he so selfish, or had someone convinced him to change his mind about her? Her heart wouldn't stop pounding.

She had been to Tambaram, where her sister-in-law Soundari lived, just once after her marriage. She couldn't remember where the house was, but she knew that Soundari's husband Ramesh had a huge travel agency right across the Tambaram bus stop. If she could get in touch with Shankar, she could clear everything up with him. He must be in some other trouble; after all, they'd been married for four years, and for years before that he had courted and wooed her, chasing her endlessly. Could all of that have changed so soon? *Anjaneya, give me some good news soon,* she prayed as she came out of the bath. She seemed to have gained some confidence at last.

6

'Serve yourself the potato poriyal. We don't make sambar like your people, though,' Ayesha said. 'There's this room we use for storage, with a few odds and ends. I will clean that up as well and give it to you. Things you need for the house, vessels, they're all here. We will buy some groceries and fill up the store, you can cook for yourself. You may feel awkward eating in our home.'

Did I know his caste or language when I fell in love with him? Did I not grow up a vegetarian, and dearly love and embrace a husband who relished his meat and fish? Shankar! How could you forget me?

Indu had lunch and called her sister-in-law on Akbar's phone. Someone picked up, but as soon as she said her name, the line was cut. After that the number was engaged. Indu felt like her chest would implode with anger. What if she just went to see them in person? As soon as this thought occurred to her, Akbar's phone rang.

Mehr picked up, and a few moments later she handed the phone to Indu saying it was for her.

It was Soundari's husband, Ramesh.

'Indu, I am calling you from outside the house. I know what has happened. Shankar is just very confused. Everyone else has confused him even more. They've taken him back to their hometown. I tried to convince him to stay, but he just wouldn't listen. It's as if my wife, our mother-in-law and father-in-law all have him under their spell, and he's utterly confused.'

'Anna, he loved me, fought with everyone and married me. Has he forgotten all that? When I told him yesterday that I left unscathed, he was so happy. Would anyone lie about these things? If even he doesn't believe me, then...' She choked, unable to finish the sentence. 'Should I go to Dindigul? If Shankar sees me in person everything will be alright, he will be fine. One thing is for sure, if Soundari or his mother and father try to create any further confusion I won't let this go so easily. I will gather everyone in town and ask for justice. I have been given an appointment with the Chief Minister next week. If I utter one word, all of you will be in jail.'

'Don't do that, Indu! Don't go to Dindigul. That will create a lot of problems. Please be a little patient, ma. I'll keep an eye on whatever's going on there. A friend of mine is related to a senior police officer. I'll consult him once, ask him what to do and get in touch with you. Don't rush this,' he said. 'Don't let anyone know that I am helping you. This is my cell phone number. Call me whenever you want to. Stay brave.' He hung up.

For some time after the call Indu remained silent. Then she took off the bangles she was wearing and her wedding chain.

'Can you help me sell these so I can get some money?' she asked, trying to hand Ayesha the jewellery.

'Indu, what's the hurry now? I can give you 5,000 rupees in cash. Keep an account of everything, and we'll settle it later. Now wear your jewellery.' Ayesha refused to touch the bangles and chain. She then asked Akbar to hand Indu 5,000 rupees.

Indu took the money sheepishly and, without meeting Akbar's eyes, said, 'I will return this very soon.'

'Eating until your stomach's full can make all that fear go away,' Ayesha had said earlier. Indu had taken heed and eaten everything Ayesha had served her. Talking to her brother-in-law after that meal had given her some more strength. She felt a little better. Ayesha switched on the air conditioner in Indu's room and asked her to sleep. Thick curtains blocked out the harsh noon sun. For three days she hadn't slept a wink. At last, this new hope and confidence brought her some sleep.

7

Jameela came enquiring, 'Ayesha, are you well?' Ayesha got up and embraced her childhood friend.

'What have you brought from Dubai? Is this bangle new? Looks very good,' Jameela said, stroking the bangle around Ayesha's wrist.

'Yeah, sure, and she's brought a ten-sovereign gold chain for you,' Mehr mocked as she left the room.

Jameela's face shrank.

'Mehru, what are you saying?' Ayesha yelled at her daughter, and then said to her friend, 'I was just thinking of you today when I was eating mutton kulambu. Stay here with me for four days and make food me, won't you? Eating all that bland biryani has made my taste buds go numb.'

As the two old girlfriends sat reminiscing, gossiping about this and that, a little boy came looking for Jameela, asking her to come home.

'My grandson Jaffer. He's studying in a convent,' Jameela said before lowering her voice. 'My life, it's becoming more pathetic as the years roll by. His mother is my own younger brother's daughter. I took pity on their state and married her off to my son. I deserve this and more. My son? He pretends to not hear anything that goes on in that house of mine. My daughter-in-law doesn't like it even if I leave the house for a short while. Ayesha, find me a job in Dubai. I work like a dog here, and what respect do I get in return?' Her eyes were moist.

'You are old now. They won't give you a job. Nor will they give you a visa. Even I am not planning to go there now.' Ayesha got up and went into her room. She emerged with a plastic bag. Handing it over to the boy, she said, 'Give this to your mother. Tell her that I said Petha will come back home later.'

The boy broke into a bright smile as he looked inside the bag, then nodded at Ayesha and ran home.

Jameela wrapped the loose end of her saree tightly around her head and went into the kitchen saying she'd make cardamom tea for her friend. Mehru caught her mother alone then and asked, 'Why are you asking everyone you see to come and stay in the house, ma? This old hag is quite the character. Keep an eye on all the things at home.'

'Will you keep quiet, Mehru,' Ayesha reprimanded her daughter.

Sitting on the floor and talking at leisure with her girlfriend had given Ayesha much pleasure, and her heart was happy. Indu finally woke up from her nap, washed her face, and joined the women. Jameela handed her a cup of tea.

When the officer called to check in on her, Indu briefly explained her predicament to him. He too felt that a police complaint was not the right move just then. 'We will talk and solve this problem,' he said. Just as he hung up, Ramesh called again.

This time Indu didn't beat around the bush. She laid her threat bare: she wouldn't think twice about doing something drastic.

Ramesh asked her to call him back in ten minutes. When she did, he pretended they hadn't been speaking, asked her how she was doing, and handed the phone to his wife.

'Anni, where has he gone?' Indu asked her sister-in-law.

Soundari, her voice dripping with feigned innocence, said, 'He didn't tell me anything properly, Indu. Out of the blue, he vacated his house, dumped everything in our home, and went off again. Poor thing, he seemed very shaken. We tried to talk to him, but he's acting like he's gone a bit mad. This morning Appa finally called to let me know that he's gone home to Dindigul.'

'Anni, I am going to meet and talk to the CM next week. Just tell your brother that. Tell him this too: the girl he ran behind, the one he fell in love with and married, wouldn't lie to him. If something had happened to me, I would have died right there. But now, if anyone here thinks they can cheat me and get away with it I will not spare them,' Indu warned and hung up right away.

Five thousand rupees in hand, nearly ten pounds of gold on her, she was confident that she would do just fine for the moment. First, she needed to go to her old university and submit an application for duplicate certificates. Then she'd have to go to the computer centre and get some proof of education from them as well. She would handle whatever came her way. As Shankar's face appeared in her mind again, that familiar old thought—*how could he do this to me*—came back to haunt her, and her heart sank. More agony.

'Is there a temple somewhere near here?' Indu asked.

Ayesha cut in just as Jameela began to tell her that Ponniyamman Temple was nearby. 'Not there, there's a Ganesha temple. You know Noor Mohammed who has a shop in Little Mount? His son-in-law has sent a letter with me. Indu needs to be shown the temple, and then this letter has to be delivered. Will you send your grandson to run this errand, Jameela? On the way back he can bring Indu home?'

'I'll go myself. I owe Noor 50 rupees though,' Jameela said sheepishly. Ayesha looked around to make sure no one else was in sight, reached for the little purse she'd tucked into her waist-band, fished out a 50 rupee note, and handed it to her.

'Golden girl, who has a heart like yours?' Jameela began. Ayesha signalled to her to stop when Mehr entered the room.

Jameela understood, and changed the conversation quickly. 'You know you don't have to go all the way to the main road to go to Little Mount now. Just beyond the temple there's a small concrete pathway. Cars can't use it, it's too tiny. But a cycle or bike can. It's pretty easy to come and go from Little Mount,' she said as she adjusted the pallu around her head.

As the two women prepared to leave, Ayesha handed over two plastic bags filled with goodies and two letters, saying, 'Noor's son-in-law has sent this for his wife and child. Poor boy, he left for Dubai ten days after his nikkah, it's now been four years. She's even had his child here, but he hasn't been able to visit. He's going mad all alone there. The rules say he needs to be sent home every two years and must be given days off, but his employer hasn't done any of that. Look at what we have to do for the sake of these stomachs of ours!' Ayesha sighed. Then she looked at Indu, who was standing by the gate, and said to her friend, 'Jameela, that girl is already crumbling, don't ask her anything about her life now.'

8

The two women left Ayesha's home and made their way to the temple, crossing many bungalows and new apartment buildings on the way. Indu liked that there were many trees along the streets.

'I can't quite believe this is Chennai. Looks like Bangalore, no? I didn't even know this neighbourhood.' She breathed in the scent of trees bursting with flowers.

'Of course, ma. Once you've lived here you won't like living anywhere else. See, behind Saidapet Court there's only one road that goes in and out. On this side is Anna Poriyal College. On that side is the Adyar River. Behind us is Kotturpuram. But you can't go to any of these places. There's a large wall that separates us from them. There's not much crime here either. But we get too many monkeys from the college.'

Indu couldn't help but smile when she heard Jameela say poriyal—stir-fried vegetables—instead of the Tamil word for engineering, poriyiyal. Looking around, she asked, 'Monkeys? For real? In this city?'

'You can't see them after dark. But early in the morning they'll begin their attacks on everything,' Jameela said. 'There's even a hillock here.'

'A hillock too?'

'Yes, Little Mount, that's the name of the bus stop as well. You see these two streets? The hillock is behind them, probably as tall as a three- or four-storey building. There's a church at the top. The neighbourhood has a lot of Christians.'

'Take me there one day, Jameelamma,' Indu said, and then asked, 'What is that scent? It's such a striking fragrance.' She looked up at the tall handsome tree in front of them.

'This tree's flower... Wait, what's it called? Your people use it as an offering to God,' Jameela said, and asked the man standing inside the compound wall to pick up a flower and give it to her. Some petals had fallen off, but when she opened the flower that had closed in on itself she said, 'This is nagalingam. Look, it looks like a lingam.'

'This is pretty special. I think this may be the first time I am seeing this flower on a tree,' Indu said.

'What are you saying? Really? I'll bring you fresh flowers from this tree tomorrow morning. You know, two decades ago herds of deer roamed around here? From the college, the grounds of the Governor's Bungalow, and Guindy National Park beyond them—deer from all these places would jump across the river to visit us. Now they have built a large wall across that path. It used to look like a forest, you know, thick trees and all. They say they are building apartments there now and chopping trees down by the dozen. This neighbourhood is made up of just about four or five streets, and most of the homes were five- and six-ground bungalows. Some of them are being torn down and turned into apartment buildings. Behind this is Rangarajapuram. Look, this is the movie star Lakshmi's house. That's Meena's house. A lot of movie stars live here.' Indu reached the temple listening to Jameela's lesson on local history.

'It's 6.30 now. I will come back in an hour. Don't go anywhere. Pray in peace and wait right here,' Jameela said and went on her way to run her errand.

9

The temple had a new gopuram, and it looked to Indu as if the main idol had been recently consecrated. She gently slapped both her cheeks in prayer. The space was clean, large and peaceful. Across the entrance was the Vinayagar shrine, Perumal to his right; to the left, a shrine for Shiva and Shakti, and a little behind them Murugan with Valli and Deivanai. On one side were the nine planets, and then, finally she saw the small Hanuman idol.

'Anjaneya! I have prayed to you all my life. I have taken every major life decision in your temple. Shankar must have a change of heart and come back to me. He must accept me. He must believe that nothing happened to me.' She walked around the shrine in prayer. After her circumambulation, she found a quiet corner in the main temple hall and sat down. By 7.30 p.m. the temple began to empty. She got up and walked to the entrance, and under the glow of a street lamp in the distance she spotted Jameela's floral saree-veil.

'Did you pray to your heart's content? Everything will be alright soon, don't you worry,' Jameela said as she walked swiftly over to Indu.

'Are you related to Ayeshamma?' Indu asked.

'No, ma. We are childhood friends. Ayesha is an only child,' Jameela said. 'Her mother married her off to a relative. You've seen Ayesha's face, no? It's like that because of smallpox. One of her eyes is also smaller than the other. Her husband Amjad Ali came under pressure from his elders, agreed to the nikkah with her, gave her two children and then left her. You know this place called Nidur? It's near Mayavaram. He's married someone from there and has four other children now. One thing I can say with confidence, Ayesha's mother was truly a brave woman. Ayesha found a job in Dubai and began to send all her money here. With that money Ayesha's mother built this house, brought her grandchildren up well, gave them the best education, sent them to work, got her granddaughter married off. She did it all by herself. That's when this man tried to come back into their lives, into that house. The old woman just wouldn't allow it. She passed away two years ago, poor thing. Look, Ayesha told me about your problem. Everything will be fine, don't you worry. Ayesha's got a beautiful heart. She will do everything to help you. She smiles despite all of her troubles and doesn't show the world everything that's weighing her down. Ayesha's one of a kind.' Jameela's words comforted Indu.

'Ameera...?' Indu began, and Jameela interjected, 'That girl! Poor thing thought she could sacrifice her life for her family and went to Dubai to marry some old man. We tried to stop her; you see, nobody does these things where we are from, but she just wouldn't listen. Her brother Yousuf even threatened to drink rat poison to stop her. She has two younger sisters, and Yousuf could never hold on to a job, so Ameera was very stubborn about it and made everyone agree. Look at her fate! In truth, she was doing well for the first few years. They married off her two sisters then and set up a big shop near Saidapet Market. Everything was going so well when, tch...' Jameela stopped for a tense moment before continuing, 'Suddenly one day there was a call from Dubai. They said that Ameera had poisoned her husband and killed him. That the police were going to arrest her and throw her in prison. No one that knew Ameera could believe this. She can't even stand up to someone and talk to them firmly, how could she have... Allah! Poor boy, Yousuf, what could he do? Who has the money to go that far? The only soul he knew there was Ayesha. He called her and cried. Ayesha asked him not to worry and promised to help. And did she live up to her word or what!' Jameela was obviously very proud of her best friend.

Indu understood what Ayesha was made of then. Even in the midst of all the bad things that were happening to her, something good seemed to have happened. She found some peace and calm. She'd come home to a really good soul.

'Jameelamma, where are you from? Your dialect is a bit different from mine, every sound is a bit elongated.'

'Ramanathapuram. But it's been a while since I came here. Now my Tamil is more like Madras' than my district's. Both my family and Ayesha's speak Tamil, Ameera's speaks Urdu. I'd say even their Urdu has many Tamil words.'

Indu looked around as Jameela filled her in. She wanted to find a job quickly and then maybe a small house to rent in this neighbourhood. It was a really good place. But where were the shops?

'Listen, aren't there any stores around here?'

'See, this side is Adyar, you go to the other side and you'll reach Saidapet Bazaar. You go further and you are in T Nagar itself, you'll get everything there. Also, four of our people have stores in Rangarajapuram. Look, this is Srinivasa Market, and behind this there's a Sri Shoppe. Even there you'll get whatever you need to run the house.' Jameela kept singing the neighbourhood's praises.

10

Mehru sat next to her mother. Akbar had laid his head down on his mother's lap. Ayesha held Mehru's hands in one of her own, and with the other she gently ruffled her son's hair. Her grandson was watching television and her granddaughter was sleeping in a cradle close by. A comfortable home, her kin nearby. Content, she wanted to live like this for the rest of her days.

'Umma, do you still have your visa or did you cancel it?' Her daughter's voice pulled her out of the world of thoughts. Before she could respond, her grandson shouted from the entryway that people from the jamaat had come to see Ayesha.

'They are laying the floor of the mosque and have asked for a donation,' Akbar explained.

'I'll give them 500 rupees, but I have to encash a draft to get the money. Ask them to come in four days,' Ayesha said.

'What? 500? Does that even befit our status? We have to give at least 10,000 to look good. I have already given them my word.' Ayesha was taken aback by the stern tone in which Akbar delivered his order.

'Do you think we are rolling in riches with no expenses? Look here, raasa, did your mother work in some company in Dubai and earn crores and crores? Didn't you say we have to pay the home loan too? A thousand rupees will do!' she said.

'Salaam alaikum,' she heard someone say. Ayesha wrapped her saree around her head firmly and opened the curtain to the entryway saying, 'Alaikum salaam.' She sat them all down and asked Mehr to make tea for everyone.

They talked about this and that for a long time, all the gossip from town, stories from Dubai, and then when the word 'donation' made its way into the conversation in that sing-song drawl, she said she had to go to the bank and asked them to come back in two days to collect a thousand rupees.

Just a thousand? They looked at Akbar in shock when Ayesha told them she wasn't going back to Dubai anymore. Mehr came back with tea. They drank it in silence and went their way.

'Why are you going around telling everyone that you won't go back to Dubai anymore?'

Ayesha's face fell when she heard that same harshness in his tone once again.

'Akbaru, why are you shouting now? Tell her what's really going on in a way that she can understand,' Mehru reprimanded.

Akbar collapsed into a chair and sat quietly. As Mehru began to talk, it became clear to Ayesha that as soon as her mother had died, her husband had renewed his relationship with her children. Some MLA from Nidur wanted to marry his daughter off to Akbar. It had all been arranged by the man who had suddenly become a father to them.

'They are very well off. They came and asked for his hand. The girl is educated, she went to Trichy College. Looks very beautiful. Car, bungalow, they have a lot of riches. One daughter, four brothers,' Mehru reeled off the details. Ayesha heard it all in silence.

'They are so wealthy... They are a bit hesitant only because I have no property or wealth in my name. So, you know, this house, in my name...'

Ayesha interrupted before Akbar could finish his sentence. 'That's fine! We will do it, what is there? I will register the house in your name. Let Mehru live upstairs for as long as I am alive. If she wants, let her pay some nominal rent. We should all live together.'

No one said anything for a while.

Finally, when Akbar found his voice, he said, 'Umma, the girl is from such a rich family. Someone or the other will keep coming to see her. If the upstairs portion is empty that will suit us well. Now you know why I said that when the house beside us goes on sale, we should buy it.'

If he could tell her that it didn't suit him to live in the same house as his sister, he could tell her that it didn't suit him to live with his mother too. She knew what Mehrunnisa was like. If she didn't get half of Ayesha's wealth there would be hell to pay. Ayesha was certain that the upstairs portion of the house was for the daughter and the downstairs portion was for the son. But at that point she decided that she would not tell her children that her mind was made up, that she wouldn't go back to Dubai.

'Look, ma, what if we do this? You have a lot of jewellery, right? You sell it all and give me the money, my husband and I will buy a house somewhere else,' Mehru suggested. Before Ayesha could respond to all this, Jameela walked past all of them and went into the kitchen. She had heard it all, and Jameela wanted to somehow tell Ayesha that her husband had been scheming with these kids.

While the rest of the family was watching television, Ayesha walked to the backyard. Jameela was looking at the winners list of the day's lottery.

'How many lakhs did you win?' Ayesha joked, and then she reprimanded Jameela, 'You are going to ruin your eyesight. Why don't you read sitting under the tubelight?'

A vexed Jameela said, 'As if I'm going to win.' Then she lowered her voice. 'Ayesha, this is your family matter, but I have to tell you this: don't just give everything away and become an orphan like me.'

Mehru, who'd quietly come to listen to them talk, yelled, 'You old hag, what are you telling my mother now?'

Akbar heard the noise and came out, and from the way Mehru was yelling he understood what had happened. Jameela tried to come up with an excuse to make peace.

But Akbar was angry. 'You first leave our home. Don't you try to sour things between us children and our mother.'

Before Jameela could say anything Mehru held her by the shoulder and shoved her towards the gate.

As she walked away Jameela shouted, 'Ayesha, these two aren't speaking on their own. They are parroting what that man who abandoned you to the roads has taught them.'

Akbar got up to hit Jameela. Ayesha held his hands and stopped him. Jameela ran screaming down the road even as all the neighbours watched, and her son and daughter-in-law came out of their home.

When she found out what had happened, Jameela's daughter-in-law yelled, 'Why the hell did you go to their home?'

Now Ayesha came running to defend Jameela and calm everyone down.

'This is how the new rich act, don't we all know just how she made her money?'

Jameela jumped on her daughter-in-law to stop her from making wild allegations against Ayesha. Her son came in between them, and in the commotion the old woman fell down. Ayesha quietly returned home, unable to see her friend hurt anymore.

Akbar was waiting for her at her door. 'Why do you insist on keeping all this riffraff around you? We are better than them, don't you see, ma?' he sulked.

Mehrunnisa came up from behind him. 'The two of them were talking about going to the theatre to watch a Rajinikanth movie. When I told them I'd get them a CD, that they could watch it at home, they said that going to the kottai to watch it is part of the movie experience, otherwise it won't be satisfying. What do you say to that? Ammi doesn't even understand that you have to act rich when you have wealth,' she whined.

Ayesha went into her room to lie down.

Indu heard it all. Her resolve to leave the house became stronger. The siblings would surely throw her out onto the road if she didn't, like they had Jameela. She began to make a list in her head, of all the things she needed to do, starting the next day, to find a job.

11

Ameera finished her evening prayers and lay down on the straw mattress Anni had given her. She could hear Anni speaking in a low voice through the door. Anni hadn't changed at all. Whenever you went to bed you'd have her voice for company, she'd constantly be saying something. Her annan, on the other hand, would say nothing. The longer her nightly chattering went on, the more you could hear its echoes in his actions the next morning.

She heard her infant nephew crying and picked him up and placed him on her lap, patting him gently. His name was also Saif. Ameera felt as if her own child was nearby.

What is my son doing now? Who's taking care of him? Those demonesses. They'll lash out against that innocent child now that they can't do anything to me. He'll pay the price for being my son. Allah!

She cried for her son who'd been orphaned even though she was alive. What strange laws. She sighed because she knew her reality. She had no choice but to forget that child.

The baby slept as Ameera's soft hands patted him gently. She leaned against the wall. She could tell that the state of the house was better than it had been when she'd left. Anni had quite a bit of gold on her hands and around her neck. This had been a one-room house once. Now there were two bedrooms and there was an upstairs portion too, which they'd rented out. Even though she knew and Anni knew that it was all possible because of Ameera's remittances, for which she kept no account, Anni spoke as if it was all because of how well her brother's shop was doing.

Anni Parveen was quite pleasant when she first married Ameera's brother. But as the years rolled by, she began to treat his sisters like dirt. He was hopelessly henpecked. It was his cowardice that sent Ameera to Dubai. No job, no money. Even if he had money, Anni wouldn't have let her husband give them anything. Ameera had thought he would at least marry their sisters off if she married an old man and sent money home.

When she was younger, there was talk of marrying Ameera to Anni's brother Irshad. But things changed when, one day, Anni was invited to Hyderabad for a friend's wedding. They'd known of the family's financial situation and had even sent tickets.

Irshad was not like Anni. He was a good man. Poor thing, how broken he was when he found out she wasn't to be his. Even though they had never spoken to each other, their eyes had often met and spoken the language of affection. Ameera had made up her mind to marry Irshad, but Anni had come back from the wedding with an old woman who kept staring at Ameera, and Ameera couldn't figure out why at first. When she finally found out, Ameera agreed without any fuss. Even though all of their people, everyone in their neighbourhood, came to dissuade her, to tell her that this just wasn't their custom and that she must say no to this wedding, Ameera thought to herself that her beauty could buy her two sisters and her brother's family a good life, and so for all of their sakes she married a sixty-year-old man.

Irshad first. Then Sheikh Mubarak Ali. Who might enter her life next? Her Anni was no fool, she was sure to find a way to sell Ameera's good looks once again in the marriage market. Even if Ameera met the Chief Minister and asked him for a job, they'd stop her from going out, saying she was an uneducated fool. She didn't like the idea of living with another man.

She remembered Mubarak Ali's tender love. Ameera thought of the two years she lived in his palace like a queen, and then the four years of darkness during which she saw no future, in jail, wondering what awaited her next. *Allah.*

12

The image of her son shoving her friend and not even allowing her to speak flashed before Ayesha's eyes all night. Even when she was penniless, Jameela had ensured that Ayesha's children had food. To Ayesha, Jameela was no less than a sister, the only person she trusted other than her own mother. Her children seemed to be full of themselves, thanks to her newly acquired money; they were forgetting their past. She was also worried about their new relationship with the man who'd abandoned her. If only her mother were around. She'd never have let something like this happen. No one dared act against her word or will.

Just some hours ago when her son and daughter had asked her for her property and jewels, she had been ready to give it all to them, but should she, after all she'd seen? The doubt took a strong hold of her.

She'd worked hard for thirty years. Akbar was sure to lose his temper if she told him she didn't want to work anymore. She just did not have the strength in her body or mind to go back to Dubai and labour. Maybe if she spoke to her son-in-law she could solve this problem. He was a good man. Thinking of him gave Ayesha some confidence. Inshallah, she was no stranger to troubles of this, or any, kind. Whatever happened, happened.

In the end, all three women who had landed in Chennai thinking all their troubles were over couldn't sleep a wink as they worried about their futures.

13

The next day Indu began running around to get her hands on duplicate certificates from the institutes she'd studied in. Her period was worse than usual, because of the tremendous stress her body and mind were under. She didn't have enough money to go see a doctor. There was no news from the government officers. The days kept rolling by and Indu didn't know what to do next. But Ayesha stayed true to her word; she emptied the storeroom, bought groceries and gave Indu the things she needed to live alone. That had been a source of relief.

The money she had in hand was fast disappearing. She had to rely on her jewels next. When she took her wedding chain off, memories of the man who'd tied it around her neck began to haunt her. She strung her wedding pendant onto a black bead chain she'd bought for forty rupees at a roadside shop in Pondy Bazaar, fastened it around her neck, then asked Ayesha to help her sell her wedding chain. Ayesha understood Indu's circumstances and had her regular goldsmith come home and buy it.

Once every few days, Ramesh called Indu and kept her informed about goings-on at his end. When he found out she was short on cash, he sent her money. Indu was happy to have at least him on her side. Ayesha, though, refused to take even a paisa for the things she'd done for Indu.

After Ameera pressed her a few times, Indu went to meet her, and the two women called the officers to find out about meeting the Chief Minister. He had too many appointments, so theirs had been pushed. The officers didn't commit to helping the two women find jobs either.

Indu finally lost it when Ramesh called her soon after she'd heard the disappointing news from the Chief Minister's office.

'If you don't let me come and talk to Shankar's parents, I'm going to the police station to complain. I see no other way out of this. How long can I stay here?'

Ramesh said his usual piece, asking her to stay patient and telling her that he'd go and speak to Shankar's parents on her behalf.

Without access to her degree certificates, Indumathi could only find a job in a clothing store in T Nagar for 5,000 a month. She was exhausted from taking clothes off the racks and showcasing them to the endless crowds that poured into the shop from nine in the morning until nine at night.

14

Ayesha's gentle refusal to part with her wealth right away had made the house uncomfortably quiet. When she spoke to her son-in-law Shahul Hameed about it, he was utterly embarrassed and said that it had all happened without his involvement. He apologised to her and then in front of everyone at home shouted his wife down. Shahul finally left home alone when Akbar responded to his advice with contempt. Mehrunnisa didn't leave with Shahul; her excuse for staying back was that the kids didn't have school.

When Indu came home from work that night Ayesha was waiting for her at the door.

'I think something's wrong; your husband's sister and her husband called this morning. I told them you were at work but they said someone at the store picked up the phone and didn't respond clearly. You first find out what happened.'

Indu called Tambaram.

Two rings and someone picked up.

'Indu, Shankar has written a letter and run away from home, ma. It says he's going somewhere far away, where we cannot find him,' her sister-in-law said, blowing her nose. Indu stood there speechless.

Ramesh then said, 'They've admitted his mother to the hospital. Soundari is going tomorrow morning. You go and see her as well, Indu.'

But Soundari intervened, 'Don't go there now, Indu. She's a village woman, you know what she's like, she'll run her mouth and just won't calm down. What do you say?'

'Anni, did you register a complaint with the local police station?' Indu asked, her throat nearly closing up in grief.

'No, Indu, we are searching for him. We'll see. Don't get scared now, you have to be brave, okay?'

Ayesha figured out what had happened and took the phone from Indu and spoke to them.

Was Shankar really just a coward, or did he love her too much? Ramesh had said that when Shankar thought of the unspeakable things they might have done to her in the brothel, he began to go a little mad. Indu stopped being angry with Shankar and understood that he was acting out because he'd loved her too much.

'Anna! Let's place an advertisement in the papers. What if I publish one saying nothing happened to me?'

'No, don't do that, ma. More people will ask him about it. You know what he's like, what if he does something to himself when everyone finds out just what happened to you? For now, we have sent people out to search for him. He will come back on his own, you wait and see,' Ramesh said.

Indu felt that he was right. She spent her days pleading and praying to the gods for her husband's return once again. Every time she walked on the road, she looked for him.

Since she had to stand all day at work, her health began to worsen. Stopgap meds would no longer work; the gynaecologist had told her she'd have to have a D and C. Where would she go for the money?

Soundari called to tell Indu that her mother was still pretty unwell. She'd asked a private investigator to look for Shankar and bring him home. An oracle back in the village had predicted that in a week's time everything would be resolved, she added. Indu began to feel more confident in her faith that Shankar would come back and accept her and they'd go back to living their lives like before. She continued with her prayers, her fasting and her temple visits with this renewed hope.

15

Laughter and conversations spilled over from the backyard. In the movie playing on the television, Senthil was acting like Rajinikanth. The gathering clapped.

'Mehr Amma, how long it's been since we watched a movie together. Let's all go?' Maragatham asked.

'Let's go, let's go,' Ayesha said, and everyone began to make a list of the new movies.

When Jameela said that the new Rajini movie was doing well, everyone agreed that that was the one they'd go watch.

'You find out how many people are coming and let the grocer Muhammed know, he'll book the tickets. Jameela will also come. But my kids won't,' Ayesha said. This was the first time Ayesha was seeing Jameela after that day. *It's my house, I built it with my money, who are they to ask Jameela not to come here*? She'd been enraged.

When she went back into her home, Ayesha was shocked to see the man she'd once married sitting in her living room with her children. When her mother had been around he'd been scared to even be seen on their street; now, he was inside the house! All because of her children and their antics. She grew irate as she looked at him.

She walked into the house without speaking to him, but sat at the entrance to the kitchen so she could hear what they were talking about. As she heard him speak, she began to feel flustered again. The hospitality her children were showing this man made her very angry. He seemed to be doing way better than before. He was making a living as an assemblyman's PA. His two children were studying to become engineers. He claimed that the new wife had been his lucky charm, and that he'd bought two homes in Mayavaram. He just wouldn't stop showing off. What he really meant was that he hadn't come for Ayesha's money. When he loudly said, so that she would hear it, that he had come to do something good for his children, Ayesha just could not stop herself from laughing.

When he'd abandoned her and run away, he had an unsettled bill at the tea shop for 150 rupees. While she was struggling to give her children food even once a day, the tea shop bhai had come home and made a big scene. That was when she had begun working for that good Telugu tailor lady, stitching saree falls and hooks for blouses. She'd get five or ten rupees a day. She had given bhai ten rupees every month to pay off that debt. What were her children doing listening to him run his mouth now?

'Akbaru, that's enough, ask him to get up and leave now. He left me alone with two tiny babies and ran behind another woman. You may have forgotten, but I won't forget it until I breathe my last,' Ayesha yelled from inside.

'Look, ma! Don't go into all those old stories now. He's cried to Akka and me many times about what he did, that he wasn't thinking straight when he did all that. Now he's arranging my wedding with this big family. It's not enough that we have money. We need status too. What have you decided about the house? You think I'm going to abandon you on the streets?' Her son's clever line of questioning did a number on her blood pressure.

'Status, ah? Your mother had to even wash that rich old sheikh lady's buttocks in Dubai to buy this property. Does he know that? You're already talking like this, who's to tell, you might even find your old mother ugly once you marry into all that wealth. If it's a marriage proposal from people who understand our reality, then okay. Otherwise let's look for someone else,' Ayesha said with finality.

When her husband tried to talk to her, she became more enraged.

'That man is the reason for everything that's gone wrong with us. Ask him to leave now.'

Amjad Ali signalled something to his son and left the house.

'Then I am also going. Keep all your wealth to yourself and live alone with it,' Akbar told his mother.

'Go, why don't you, go away!' Ayesha screamed and then began to hiccup. She pushed aside the glass of water her daughter brought her. Soon enough her blood pressure and diabetes had their way. Ayesha felt faint and then fell.

Her flustered children brought in the neighbourhood doctor, who asked them, 'What medication is she on?' Akbar and Mehr had no idea.

He wrote a prescription, gave her an injection, and told them to bring her to the hospital for tests. He then told her to get some sleep. 'Keep her calm and stable,' he said.

Ayesha had regained consciousness but didn't open her eyes.

'Akka, if something had happened that man would have also come asking for his share. She hasn't written a Will, right...' Mehr must have signalled to Akbar not to say anything because he stopped his sentence midway. Did this mean that they even let their own father into their home out of selfishness? Of course they'd inherit their father's trait. Ayesha felt like laughing in frustration.

When she opened her eyes and sat up, Akbar and Mehr spoke to her nonchalantly, insisting she rest. They then left her alone in the room.

She got up slowly and switched on the television in the living room. She sat in front of it, but her mind was elsewhere. In the few days she'd been back home Ayesha had understood her children well. Still, listening to Akbar speak so unashamedly made her heart ache. Ayesha thought of the advice her Umma had given her many times. *Don't agree to buy them everything they ask for right away.*

'Isn't it all my fault then?' When thirteen-year-old Mehr demanded 4,000 rupees so she could go to Jaipur on a school trip, and when Akbar asked for a bike as soon as he joined college, were these things not given to them right away? Whenever they spoke to me on the phone, they'd only ask for this or that. Wasn't the same thing happening now? She thought she should just give it all to them and disappear somewhere far away.

The house was completely silent. Ayesha didn't speak to anyone, though she did watch everything going on around her, calculating her next move. After she took her night pills, she gave it some thought and popped a sleeping pill. As she closed the medicine cabinet, her mind lingered on the pills for a second. But the next moment she said to herself, 'What is this thought!' and slapped herself on the head.

'Ya Allah! Forgive me for thinking of sin,' she prayed.

16

Even though Ameera knew her brother was useless, she begged him to do something. She cried to her sister-in-law that she didn't want another marriage, but that was of no use either. She asked the few people who came home to visit her for help, but they did nothing to stop the wedding. *Remarriage is allowed*, they tried to explain to her. But the fact that she didn't like the look on the face of the man Anni had found her didn't seem to move anyone. Ameera knew that Anni couldn't stand her beauty. This was Anni's revenge.

As she stood kneading dough for the night's chapatis, she heard Anni call out to her. She repositioned her head scarf and peeped out through the curtain, and knew right away what was going on as she spotted the man standing with her sister-in-law.

'Here, he's brought some sweets. There's a mixture in the thooku chatti. Bring a plate of snacks. And some water,' Anni said.

The way he looked at her made Ameera shudder. He'd been coming baring his teeth for four or five days, and the other day he'd even tried to cross the line with her and had run away when she'd picked up the vegetable knife. The fact that he'd come back meant that Anni had emboldened him.

She heard Anni whispering to him as she stood by the curtain and knew that she'd guessed correctly after all.

Ameera brought the snacks and as she turned around to go back in, Anni said, 'Ameera, stay here, ma. You know he has a shop in Meesappettai, no? It seems he's made a good profit this year. What would you like? He wants to measure your hand for a bangle and ring,' Anni said.

Ameera went back into the kitchen saying she'd bring water, washed her hands, brought some water out, and placed it in front of them saying, 'Bhabhi, I will go to Mehru's house and come back. They said the government wants to give me some money, I'll find out about it and be back.' And without waiting for a response she left the house, got onto the road, and kept on walking.

17

Indumathi hadn't gone to work for two days. Her legs felt like worn out old pieces of cloth. Her lower abdomen felt heavy and her body felt only pain and more pain. Even if she were to go to work the next day, they wouldn't let her in. She mixed buttermilk with leftover rice, drank it, and lay down on the bare floor. As she lay there, the thought that people could betray other people like this haunted her.

Every night Akbar's English newspaper found its way into her room. That's where she'd seen an ad for a job in Vandalur. They were looking for an accountant who could handle computers. She called them up to find out more. The next morning she was there at ten. She didn't have her original certificates but did her best to explain her situation to them. Their response didn't give her any hope.

Tired, standing under the beating sun and waiting to cross the road, she looked across at the petti kadai and spotted... Shankar, in the shop. Happy, nervous, struggling to cross the road with speeding vehicles zipping past her, she noticed her sister-in-law, mother-in-law and father-in-law get out of a Tata Sumo. They seemed to be laughing. Indumathi watched as they all got into the car with cool drinks in their hands. Then she noticed the woman getting into the car with Shankar, and in an instant, she knew what had happened.

Shankar's betrayal on the one hand, and Ramesh's acting on the other... not even a single teardrop left her eyes. She knew clearly then that nothing was in her hands. She didn't have any money in hand or the strength in her being to go complain to the police. She felt this burning rage then and wanted to drag everyone who had betrayed her onto the road and insult them in every way possible. When she looked up, the strong wooden ceiling underneath the tiled roof caught her eye.

She heard a voice call out to her from Ayesha's house. 'Akka, you have a call.' She got up slowly and took the call. Ramesh. Thinking to herself she had nothing to say to him, she said, 'Tell me,' her voice betraying no emotion.

'Forgive me, Indu,' he began. 'Soundari must have found out I have been speaking to you. They seem to have plotted everything behind my back, ma, lying to me that Shankar had run away from home. She seems to be some poverty-stricken young woman. I don't know anything about her. They arranged Shankar's wedding with her without telling anyone at all. Last night he disappeared somewhere with this girl. I don't know which city or country he's gone to either...' Indu hung up before he could finish speaking.

She walked back in, closed the door, and sat down in the darkness of her sparse room. Was Ramesh being truthful or was he lying? Had he been sitting inside the vehicle? Did he see her from inside the car? Is that why he called her to tell her this made-up story? Why were humans this vile? How long could she live on Ayesha's benevolence? The way Mehrunnisa and Akbar looked at her made her shrink in shame.

For half an hour she sat there, leaning against the wall. Then a thought possessed her, and she took the paper she'd kept next to her for the purpose of writing a job application and began to write on it.

Someone knocked gently on her door. She hid the letter she was writing under a pillow and opened the door. Ameera.

18

Ameera walked in, sat on her haunches, and began to weep.

'I married the old man and went to Dubai so they could live well here. For two whole years I sent them money whenever they asked. Even before my nikkah, my bhabhi took a lot of gold and money from him as mahr. Now some guy, she says he's her mama, that man... he looks like a rogue. He comes home when no one is around and speaks very dirtily,' she sobbed.

'Remarriage is quite common in our homes, Akka. I told Bhabhi that I don't mind marrying an old man, even if he's poor, if he gives me food twice a day that's more than enough, but she just doesn't listen at all. This man is not good news. It's written all over his face that after the nikkah he won't hesitate to do as he pleases with me. For the two square meals that my bhabhi serves me I have been doing everything in the house, I work like an ox. I told her that I don't mind living like this, but she won't listen. My brother doesn't seem to care what happens to me. I can't do this anymore. They say suicide is haram in my religion, but I am going to eat something and kill myself, I have made up my mind. I don't see what else I can do now.' As Ameera said this, Indu's face hardened.

'If I stay at home and do some tailoring, I can make five rupees here and ten rupees there, save up and then buy an embroidery machine. There's good money to be made embroidering flowers on sarees. I keep telling her that there's no need for a nikkah now, just wait until the government gives us the help it has promised, but does she listen? If I just die, all these problems will go away, right?'

Indu laughed gently.

Then Ameera said, 'I am not just saying this, I swear on Saif. Just as dawn breaks tomorrow, I will kill myself.'

Indu sighed when she noticed the conviction with which Ameera said this.

'I am in the same boat. I have 400 rupees remaining. I went to Vandalur to look for a job two days ago. There I saw, with my own eyes, my husband laughing with his new bride. I neither have the strength nor the money to fight him. No relatives to help me either. I gave it a lot of thought and decided I'll hang from this ceiling, right here. But I don't want Ayeshamma to face any problems because of me, which is why I am writing to the Police Commissioner, the Chief Minister, two newspapers, and the local Saidapet police station, and one I'll keep on me.

I was writing these six letters when you knocked. I just have to shove them inside envelopes and post them.'

'Akka. Tomorrow morning that man and my sister-in-law are going out to buy clothes and jewels. My brother will be at his store. Your neighbour, Senthil Amma, will go out to pick up clothes from her customers for ironing. I will come then. Should the two of us go together to the beach and just jump...' Ameera asked, her voice breaking.

'I have thought of all these things. But if we get caught, it will end up becoming a police case,' Indu said. 'Ameera, I can't think of what else to do, just like you. Like I said, I have no relatives left to help. I fell in love and got married, and he has abandoned me like this without even saying a word. I am unwell. I don't have the money to go and see a doctor.'

'What happened to you in Dubai, Akka? Why did your husband leave you?'

'What do I tell you? We were in love for five years before we married. Both our families were against it. Despite all that opposition we got married in the Kapaleeshwarar Temple. Shankar loved me then. He wanted to go work in Dubai and live well and show off to our families. One day, as we returned from a recruitment agency, we met a lady. We were really impressed with the way she spoke to us. Later, she called and said that she could get *me* an accountant's job in Dubai. We believed her when she said that it would be easier for Shankar to get a job there if I was already there. But then…' Indu began to shake.

'When I exited the airport, the lady who got me the job was waiting for me. Srividya, she said her name was. Now I am pretty sure that couldn't have been her real name. She took me in her car to Sharjah. To a cramped apartment. There were a lot of people there. "Stay here temporarily, when you join work they will give you a better place," she said. She gave me a room of my own there. When I turned around to go to the bathroom, before Srividya closed the door to my room, I saw it, just for a brief second. Across from my room a man emerged from another room, and behind him a woman. Lord! That image, it was enough for me to figure out just what was going on in that house.

'At first, I was very flustered, but pretty soon I figured out that I'd been trapped, and that I'd have to outsmart them to get out of there. I miscarried four months after my marriage. After that I'd had fairly bad periods every month. And if I was stressed or overworked, I'd be done for. That day was no different.

'I was lying down quietly on the bed when Srividya brought food into my room. When I told her I had period problems, her face soured. "How long will it last? Why didn't you get it treated?" The questions poured out. I didn't betray any emotion and told her that I didn't have the money to get treatment. I said that it was divine luck that had brought her my way. That if I got a D and C,

I'd be fine. I figured that if I spoke too much about it, she might start to suspect that I was on to her. So I kept flattering her every now and then too. I was scared to eat her food. What if she'd mixed something into it? I said I was nauseous and didn't eat.

'I ate some pill I had on hand in front of her and told her I'd feel better if I slept. She went out. I thought I heard a fight. She came right back in and asked me to leave, and I did so without saying anything. I felt then that it might be easier to escape outside than while trapped in that home.

'She said the car park was a little distance from the building. This bulky bouncer-like guy was walking ahead with my suitcase. I walked slowly as if I was in a lot of pain. It was a crowded neighbourhood.

'I pretended to take in the sights but was trying to come up with a plan. When I said I wanted to talk to Shankar, Srividya gave me her phone. I hardly managed to say two words to him before she snatched the phone from me, spoke to him, and hung up.

'I just had my handbag with me. The man with my suitcase crossed the road and went towards the car park. Just then Srividya got a call, and she walked talking on the phone. When she tried to cross the road with the crowd that had gathered, I stayed back and started to run in the opposite direction. I ran into a big shopping complex there, but couldn't shake off the feeling that a lot of people were following me.

'A few hours before I left for Dubai someone had given us the number of a relative. Mohan Kumar who was an officer in the Indian embassy. I had his number with me in my handbag. I ran into the mall's restroom. There, I saw a few Tamil women and told them everything.

'The women called him on one of their phones. I spoke to Mohan Kumar. He understood what had happened to me right away. He asked me to wait next to the security guards outside. And if Srividya asked me to go with her, he asked me to act like I didn't know her. The Tamil women told him where the mall was.

'When I went out, I saw Srividya with two men. I ran out and stood right in front of the tall, burly security guards. I pretended to not even see Srividya, staring at my wristwatch instead. When Srividya called out to me, I yelled back in English, "Who are you?" The guards turned around to see her, and Srividya ran out of there. When the guards asked me what had happened I began to feel faint.

'I sat on the floor right there. They gave me some water to drink. Soon the shopping complex's manager, a Malayali, came out and said he'd received a call from the embassy. They'd told him what had happened. Later that day the police came with officers from the embassy. They'd busted Srividya's racket with the details I had given them. I can remember numbers pretty well. I knew her car number, the names of the shops around her building; all of this was helpful in nabbing them.

'But I don't know who said what to him, my husband clearly did not believe me when I told him I'd gotten away unscathed. I don't have the money, backing, and the strength to go to the police. It's over, Ameera.' Indu held her hands. 'I am begging you, even if you change your mind tomorrow, just don't tell anyone about this.'

'I was going to say the same thing to you,' Ameera said. 'Write a letter on my behalf too. I only know how to sign. Write that I dictated the letter and you wrote it, say that no one else is responsible for my suicide, I'll sign it.'

19

Ameera's head was unclouded when she got home. She didn't speak to anyone, did all her chores, and lay down in her corner. The kora grass in the mat she slept on was broken and poked her back. She tried to tug at the grass to pull it out of the mat, but it kept slipping out of her hands.

The house in Dubai she'd stayed in... Was it even a house? It was more like a palace. Ameera was so rich, one had only heard of such riches in stories. He took such great care of Ameera, Sheikh Mubarak. She did the same for him. Each treated the other gently, like they would a child.

The bed had a three-foot foam mattress, but it was her lap that Mubarak liked to lay in at night. A few months after marrying him, she began to more or less understand his Arabic. She'd gently soothe him to sleep. She wasn't bitter about the marriage. She did what she did so her brother would do well. That her two sisters were married to good men too made her very happy.

Whenever she called home, Anni complained about not having enough. Mubarak would send them more than she'd even asked for. She didn't know back then that all this had irked Mubarak's family. A symbol of their conjugal bliss arrived soon enough. When Ameera was pregnant, the sixty-year-old was in awe of his own manhood. He began to treat Ameera as no less than a goddess. A dadi who'd been flown down from London took care of her. When he found out it was a boy, Mubarak's pride knew no bounds. He readied a beautiful room, painted it blue, and filled it with the most expensive toys from all over, for his son Saif Ali.

The three years she lived with him, she bathed in rose water and ate out of gold plates. All of the riches of the world seemed to be at her feet. The rare diamond the size of a gooseberry that was in a necklace her husband had given her gave his other wives heartburn. Even before she could begin crying when she heard about his passing, she had been arrested by the police for poisoning him.

'She was married against her wishes.'

'She was disappointed and unsatisfied with her marital life.'

'Having to serve an old man made her poison him.'

The complaints against her began to pile up. She cried and pleaded innocence, but did anyone listen? Having served four years in jail, Ameera felt that her time there had been better than what was happening to her in her own home.

It was all too normal to remarry, but it looked like she just couldn't stop Anni from selling her off to the scoundrel.

Suicide was haram. But she saw no other way out. Ameera begged God for forgiveness.

20

The day began as usual. Her neighbours went out to pick up clothes to wash and press from their regular customers.

As soon as Ameera entered her house Indu said to her, 'I am not even able to stand today. How do we post these letters? If we post them first thing in the morning they will reach by the evening. Otherwise Ayeshamma will be in trouble.' Ameera understood Indu's predicament but was loath to go out to do it herself. She peeked out and saw the boy who worked in the provision store, Muhammad, walking past.

She called out to him and said, 'Brother, these are job applications. Please post them carefully, okay? You do it yourself, don't give them to anyone else.' Then she handed him a fifty-rupee note. Muhammad's face brightened at the sight of the note.

'I will take my cycle and post this myself, ka.' He smiled, but then he looked at the envelopes Indu had handed him and said, 'Akka, you haven't stuck stamps on these? Should I go to the Little Mount Post Office, buy stamps, and then post them there?'

'No, pa. No stamps. Just go drop them in the post box in front of Pillaiyar Temple. It's very urgent, will you go right now?'

'Right away. I will go down to let the shop owner know and then go straight to post them.' He ran away, excited.

Muhammad got to the front of the shop and announced, 'I am taking the day off. Going to watch a movie.'

'Come here, da, what movie? Where did you get the money? Why did it take you this long to go deliver groceries and come back?' Syed came out onto the road and pulled Muhammad by his ears in anger.

'That hurts, let go!' Muhammad was furious. 'I am going to watch a film with money I earned. What's it to you? Don't raise your hands at me, I'll quit.'

'You'll quit? I'm going to fire you now. I hired you because my grandfather asked me to. It hasn't even been a month since you joined and you want a day off already. A day off, eh?' Syed was about to hit Muhammad on his neck.

Ducking away, Muhammad said, 'Look, don't you hit me. That sister who's staying in Akbar's house, she gave me this to post, and fifty rupees too. Last week my vappa was here and he gave me twenty. Seventy rupees in all. See? Does it all add up? I didn't take anything from your cash box.'

'Give me the letter. I have some work in Saidapet Bazaar, I will post it. Movie, right? You can go for the evening show. Now will you take proper care of the store, sir?' Syed took all the letters from him.

'That akka asked me to post them myself. She said not to give them to anyone,' Muhammad muttered under his breath.

'People coming to the store ask me why I've employed a child who should be in school. Your vappa has sent you here to work, to stop you from loitering about like a wastrel; you want to watch a movie now is it, a movie? Your vappa cries to me that he doesn't have money to marry your sister off, and you want to spend a hundred and fifty rupees to watch movies?'

Syed looked at the envelopes and yelled at the boy, 'What is this, da? No stamps?' He then looked at the address on one of the envelopes. His face dropped. He looked at the addresses on the other letters. Leaving the store in Muhammad's care he ran to the mosque, shouting to the people inside, 'That girl staying in Akbar's house, she's written something to the police.' He waved the letters in the air.

Everyone gathered around him and began to read the letters.

21

Ayesha lost her calm seeing her husband at the door again first thing in the morning. She went back in without saying a thing, even as her son welcomed him with warmth.

When her son expressed his disappointment at her not having made up her mind, she yelled from inside, 'Who made him the arbitrator of this case?'

No response.

'I brought two kids up on my own, you think I don't know how to marry them off? Akbaru's educated. He has his own business. If they give their girl for all that, then okay. If you are going to ask me to write off the property, give you all the land… leave right now. Look, I've spoken to Iyer from the house at the end of the road and asked him to ready the documents. When I am gone, all my jewels will go to Mehr. The house will go to Akbar. Enough? If you agree to this, we'll talk further. If not, everyone can go and mind their own business. If Akbar must have this rich alliance at any cost, I hear his father has two homes, he can write one of them off in Akbar's name, ask him to do it.'

Stunned silence followed Ayesha's sharp speech. She went to the kitchen, made herself a cup of tea and drank it. There were some snacks in a box. She took a plateful and began to eat when she thought of something, stopped eating, and emptied the snacks back into the box. She went to the backyard to wash her hands and saw a goat eating a banana leaf. *Someone must have left the gate open.* She picked up a small stone and flung it at the goat. As it ran to the side, she went to close the gate and heard whispers coming from Akbar's room.

When she re-entered the house, Mehr's door was closed.

Ayesha went to her room, closed the door behind her, and sat down. What were all these secrets between those two now? She'd seen so many palace intrigues and schemes during her time at work but had never imagined that there would be fights over the few lakhs that she had made. Didn't her kids realise that seeing them doing well had made the man who'd abandoned them bitter?

Her hands and feet were sore. She had just remembered to take her blood pressure medication when her gaze once again fell on the shiny aluminium strip of sleeping pills.

She picked it up, thinking of something, but then she hid the strip in the pallu of a saree on a different shelf.

She heard someone calling out at the entrance. She heard Akbar and Mehr shouting too. Then she heard people running towards her house's entrance. She went out to see what the commotion was.

22

Indumathi's eyes were trained on the floor while Ameera, in tears, held on to Indu's shoulders, her face veiled and scared.

'These two have written suicide notes and asked Muhammad to post them. It's our good luck that Syed read the letters and brought them to us. If something like this had happened, the police would have picked all of us up.' Before the man could finish his sentence, the others around him erupted in anger. Indu teared up, feeling utterly helpless.

Yousuf made his way through the crowd asking, 'Kya ho raha hai, Ameera?' and held her hand.

'Mera haath chodo.' Ameera shrugged his hand off in anger. 'Even if not today, one day I am going to die. You are a man, are you? Siding with your wife, you sissy, betraying your own sibling, you should be ashamed.

Maami, you have to save me. Don't send me off with them.' She fell to the ground at Ayesha's doorway.

Ayesha looked at Indu, who was crying, and Ameera, who had fallen at her feet. *How could I have forgotten them? Indu wasn't well, didn't have any money, had been abandoned by all her relatives, how could I have forgotten her, lost in my own world, my own troubles?*

'What, have we built a choultry for all the orphaned donkeys in town? Akbaru, catch them all by their necks and throw them out,' Mehr ordered.

Slowly, one word from Mehrunnisa's rant entered Ayesha's heart and began to take hold of it.

'Inshallah.' She was delirious with happiness. 'Mehru, you have done something good for the first time in your life. Everyone here is my witness. I am writing off my home, my properties, and all my gold to the jamaat. I am going to sell some jewels and buy the house next door too; we'll build a hostel for orphan girls to stay here and study. Let them learn to use computers and how to tailor. Dei, Jaffar, go to the corner house and ask Iyer to come. Now. We can ready the documents.'

'All that is fine. But why should this woman be here...?' someone asked.

'When that ghastly tide in Nagapattinam, what was it called... aang... tsunami... When it took away people's homes, did our jamaat see religion before helping everyone? They did so much good without asking if the victims were Hindu or Muslim or Christian. It does not matter if a woman who's suffering is my kin, or from my religion. To me Ameera and Indu, both orphaned by circumstance, are the same. Any woman would think like this,' Ayesha said, and then she looked at someone in the crowd and said, 'Hey! Khatija! You said your aunt did not have money for even a meal, call her and ask her to come. Jameela, it's your job now to cook for everyone here.'

Akbar tried to stop Ayesha.

'Why are you blabbering away like this now? Have you lost your mind?' He grabbed her hand and tried to drag her inside.

'Take your hands off me. What was there for you three to talk about together, alone in that room? Father and children getting together to conspire against me, is it? That man cannot digest the fact that we are better off even after he abandoned us, that's why he's so restless. You don't understand this, do you? Don't you know how hard I worked to bring you up? Shouldn't you show some gratitude?

'Do you know what that man has been telling everyone? I worked in Dubai and sent lakhs and lakhs home and so he had suspicions about how I made so much money there, which is why he left me. Do you see the spin? Everyone on this street knows how I suffered to put food on the table for two years after he left. I went to that palace in Dubai to take care of an unwell old woman as an ayah. In that household, women bought gold every month, and sometimes all of them together even bought up to a hundred sovereigns of gold. Now and then they'd ask me to buy five and ten sovereigns. To them, it was loose change. They were millionaires. You'll never understand how rich those people are. It's as if their bathrooms and toilet pipes also give out gold!' As she spoke and spoke, the crowd listened with open mouths.

'They didn't think of me as just an ayah taking care of their mother though. They gave me respect. As if *I* was their mother. For Ramzan Perunaal they'd give and give. Money, things. I would send it all back. Umma would sell it and make money here. If I worked for the other women in that household, they'd tip me five and ten. You don't understand, that's how I made all this money,' Ayesha screamed even as her throat began to hurt.

Mehru tried to come close and make peace with her, but Ayesha kept going. 'I worked in a bungalow, a palace. I could never open my mouth there. But only if my eyes and ears were open could I survive there. The way you are acting with me, closing the door behind me and speaking to each other... No... I can no longer trust any of you. I am scared to even take a sip of water, what if you've mixed something in it? Akbaru, you go with that man and marry someone with status. You, Mehru, you also leave.'

But Mehr was already in tears. 'I am sorry, ma.'

Ayesha's husband, who was watching it all, realised things had gone too far. 'I will sue you and clean you out for everything and hand it to the children. If I don't do it and show you, my name is not Amjad Ali,' he yelled.

People from the crowd yelled back at him, asking him to leave. Some elders began to give Akbar and Mehrunnisa advice. The siblings realised that the crowd was entirely on their mother's side.

Left with no choice they came and stood in front of Ayesha, looking apologetic.

Ayesha knew what was on their minds. 'I married my daughter off with gold and other things: a scooter, TV, you name it. I educated Akbar and made him an engineer, and now I've even set his business up for him. That's all, my duty is over. I've said what I want to say. I earned all of this; everyone here knows that. I will stay upstairs. Mehru and Akbaru, you can come and go anytime you want to. But you will not get a single paisa from this property. When I am gone, everything I own will go to the jamaat! Let Iyer bring the stamp paper and write this out, let our elders come and sign as witnesses, only then will I even get up from this spot. Muhammadu! Get someone from the tea shop to serve tea to everyone here.' Ayesha sat down at the entrance to her house.

Mehrunnisa and Akbar didn't look up at all. Ayesha calmed down a little then, put her arms around their shoulders and once again said, 'Inshallah.'

'Indu, you will work here as a teacher, we will discuss your salary later. Free food and boarding.' Ayesha's face brightened and her tone became more cheerful. 'Ameera, what are you looking at? You also stay here now. Learn to tailor. Working with our own two hands and making some money gives us the courage to live like nothing else can. Ameera, Indu, tear these letters up first.' She handed them back. Ameera took them in her hands and tore the letters up into small pieces.

'Jameela, not just cooking, you're in charge of the house too. Manager Jameela Madam, take these two inside please,' Ayesha said.

'Ayesha!' Jameela hid her face as she laughed, happy and proud. Indu and Ameera stood there wondering if it was all real as Jameela called them in.

Indumathi then looked at Jameela and Ayesha, both of whom were asking her to go in.

Who are these people? What am I to them? Does the fact that we were all forsaken by family bind us together? The faces of all the strangers who had helped her flashed in front of her eyes. Whom should she thank? So much had gone wrong, there were so many selfish humans around her, and yet, even without her asking, there were those who had lent her their hands. Mohan Kumar, Payal Sharma, Ayesha.

Before she could follow that thought, a car came in. She heard the door open and close. It was the government officer she had met earlier. He introduced Indu and

Ameera to the two women officers who'd come with him. Indu and Ayesha heard the officers talk and couldn't stop smiling.

Ameera looked at Indumathi and smiled.

'Alhamdulillah!'

'Anjaneya.'

Khushka

The kid smiled. Rajashekar folded his hands involuntarily and let out a prayer. 'Muruga!'

That smile. It melted his heart. It was as if, on a scorching hot day, someone had poured an ice-cold glass of water on his head. It lasted for just a second though. And then it was back to status quo. Head tilted to one side, mouth at an angle, spittle dripping out, Khushka looked at Rajashekar from the corner of his eyes.

Was it Rajini's *Annamalai*? No, in that movie he played a milkman. *Arunachalam*! Yes. That was the one. He didn't know why, but Rajashekar was reminded of the image of Lord Murugan they'd shown in that film. As he thought of that image again, he looked at Khushka with some reverence.

He looked no more than six or seven, but the old man had told Rajashekar the previous day that he was, in fact, 18 years old. Rajashekar thanked God that it wasn't a girl child who had this fate.

He laughed to himself a bit. What sort of name was Khushka? The only place he'd seen it before was on boards at roadside restaurants and tea stalls. 'We Sell Khushka', they'd announce, trying to get rid of leftover biryani rice without meat. He decided he'd try eating it sometime soon.

The others were still inside the Oppiliappan Temple. Must be an auspicious day. The temple was teeming with hordes of people. Khushka had thrown a tantrum and, unable to handle him in that crowd, Rajashekar had come out with him.

The boy was staring right at him. Rajashekar took out the furry, soft shirt, brushed it against Khushka's face and spouted some gibberish—'Joo joo…' Khushka's face lit up. Would the boy smile again? Nope. No smile.

As a baby, Sunitha had loved it when he made cooing noises. Especially 'joo joo'. The thought of Sunitha brought with it worries about the 2,000 rupees he needed. Poor Aruna had to endure the horrors of poverty and his raised hand! It was wrong, he knew. How frustrating that she wouldn't understand. During the holidays, when their daughter was in Nagercoil, she had come of age. They had done all the rituals with the seeru, platters filled with all things auspicious to mark her womanhood—betel leaves, areca nuts, vermillion, turmeric, new clothes, fruits and flowers. Now she wanted the whole shindig done once more at home and to invite the people here! Where was he to go for the money? Senseless woman.

Just then he heard Khushka coo, 'Joo joo.'

'You want me to play with you, huh?' Rajashekar asked the boy and took the fluffy shirt out and gently rubbed it against his chin again. That morning when they'd stopped for bottles of mineral water in Aaduthurai, a man with fluffy, furry toys hanging from every inch of his body had hassled them to buy something. When he showed Khushka this small furry shirt, the boy had grabbed it and hugged it close.

Huffing and puffing from the heat, the old man and his wife got into the car and sat down.

'Turn the AC up. What heat! And humidity!' the old woman said. Rajashekar turned the air conditioning up and wondered if Khushka would feel too cold. He wrapped the cheap fur shirt around the boy. And then his mind drifted back to the issue at hand: money. Worries clouding his head, he leaned forward and closed his eyes.

If he could just see Swamimalai's Murugan, he was convinced he'd somehow get the money. 'Muruga,' he said out loud.

'Why aren't they here yet?' the old man asked.

'Blessed woman must be praying for her son to become "okay" tomorrow and then take over her husband's business,' the old woman said with caustic sarcasm, letting out an annoying giggle. The old man joined her in laughter. Rajashekar heard some noise from Khushka just then and turned around to look at him.

He was shaking his head vigorously, and then he started hitting himself on the head over and over again. A soft noise filled the car—kak, kak. Rajashekar wondered if the shirt was making him uncomfortable and tried to take it off. Khushka pushed his hands away. He told the old woman about it, but she didn't seem to care.

The old man peeked at the front seat and then said, 'You go look for them and ask them to come soon.' Rajashekar got out of the car and saw them coming back with the younger daughter. When he signalled to them, they rushed back to the car.

The couple took off their son's trousers, cleaned him up, and then helped him get into a fresh pair.

'Will there be an ATM in Kumbakonam? I am running a little low on cash,' Shankar said.

'There will be, sir. We can eat there at Venkataramana Lodge and then head to Tiruvaiyaru. We can rest there for an hour and then go to Alangudi. All the temples will be closed for the afternoon anyway,' Rajashekar said as he drove.

'Swamimalai?' the old woman asked.

'It's 12 now. If you eat quickly, we can see it. Then if we visit the Guru Temple in Alangudi, we'll complete the Navagraha pilgrimage. By seven I'll get you on board the bus to Chennai at Kumbakonam, sir. You can even parcel dinner for your journey home from Iyer Hotel in Ganapathi Agraharam.'

After lunch at Venkataramana Lodge and Shankar's ATM visit, Rajashekar drove towards the next temple. Shankar took the cash out of his trouser pocket and counted it. From the corner of his eye, Rajashekar could see that they were all new, magenta-coloured 2,000-rupee notes.

'This is the new 2,000-rupee note, pa,' Shankar said as he turned around to show his father the note. Khushka held his hand out too. Shankar gave Khushka the entire wad of notes, and Khushka took some of the notes and tucked them into the pocket of his shirt.

Rajashekar just needed one of those notes. These were NRIs from the USA. They were here on pilgrimage. At best, he'd get a 100-rupee tip from them. Just as these thoughts ran through his head, his eyes met those of the woman seated in the back. Eyes that gave nothing away, shallow, like a pond. He closed his eyes and said Murugan's name to himself once again.

She must be 40. But what a beauty she was. Tall, like those dancers. And those hips. Her hands and legs, long, and her whip-like hair in a braid that touched her hips. Rajashekar sighed at the vision.

He too was disappointed when they made it to the Swamimalai Temple. It was shut. All of them looked up at the gopuram and raised their folded hands in prayer.

'You women delayed us all at that Tribhuvanam with your saree-buying spree,' the old man mumbled under his breath.

Rajashekar suppressed a giggle. The old woman had bought four sarees at the store that morning, acting all along as if they were some rare objects and not commonplace sarees. She didn't pay heed when her son muttered to himself that there wasn't enough cash.

'The old hag can just wear a t-shirt like the rest of us, why does she even need a silk saree now?' Only Rajashekar heard the old man say this.

The old woman's figure was like that. She was thin as a stick but had a completely mismatched large rear end that jutted out too far. When the old man placed the 'new design' sarees that the salesman had showed them in his daughter-in-law's hands, forcing her to buy them, she ran out of the place, her hands quivering.

Rajashekar didn't want to interfere in the matters of the rich. Poor woman. Handling that son, this errant father-in-law, and the avaricious mother-in-law... It seemed the husband at least kept her happy. She looked well-bred, and educated too.

After a heavy lunch, just as everyone was dozing off, the little girl whined, needing to go to the toilet.

'Let's go to Tiruvaiyaru, the bathrooms will be cleaner there,' Rajashekar said, and that only made the girl increase the tempo of her whining. This had been the problem with the girl the previous day too. Whenever they showed her a toilet she said, 'Sheesh, it's so dirty,' and when they asked her to go behind a tree, she said,

'Aiyo!' and continued whining. Rajashekar stopped the car.

Finally, without a toilet in sight, the girl and her mother got out of the car and went behind a tree. On their return, when the old man pulled at the granddaughter, saying something with a smile plastered across his face, the mother pulled the girl back.

'Come this way,' she said, gritting her teeth. The two went up to the other door and got in.

Even though he knew that money was not everything, Rajashekar's mind wandered back to the crisp notes tucked under the boy's fluffy shirt.

The road leading to Alangudi was filled with hay. He had to drive slowly so it wouldn't get caught in the tyres. This delayed their temple visit and the journey back to Kumbakonam. The bill was paid en route. He received a 200-rupee tip. By the time they reached the bus stop, the bus to Chennai was leaving. When Rajashekar honked, it stopped briefly.

Everyone prepared to get off. Rajashekar pushed the furry shirt down with his left hand and quietly kicked it to the back of the seat. The couple picked up Khushka and sat in the bus. The others picked up all the luggage and shuffled into the bus in a hurry.

'Joo joo...' Khushka was saying repeatedly inside the bus. Everyone else was in a hurry; no one noticed him. Rajashekar stood quietly.

Khushka looked at him from the window and screamed loudly this time, 'Joo joo!' He was moving his hands about vigorously and shaking his head. Everyone in the bus turned around and looked at the boy as the screaming and shaking increased.

Unable to see the boy suffer like that, Rajashekar banged on the side of the bus, getting the driver to stop, and then ran to the car. When he took the shirt back to the bus and handed it up through the window, Khushka smiled. That same divine smile. Just as he said Murugan's name to himself, in prayer, his fingers grazed the 2,000-rupee notes peeping out of the shirt's pocket.

Success

The old man looked like an eagle. His face wasn't wrinkled, his back wasn't bent, he wasn't even that old. Poverty, that's what had made him look like that.

Memories old and new exhausted him. There was hardly anyone at the Thiruvizhandhur Parimalanadhar Temple. It never had much patronage to begin with. Now that everyone had TVs, the norm was that, as soon as the evening lamp was lit, you sat in front of that damn box.

His nose itched without snuff powder. Not a single paisa in hand. If the old Iyengar man came, he would ask for snuff money; that man got a handsome pension, he could give him some.

The old man raised his hand above his eyes to look out expectantly, awaiting Iyengar. No one was out there. Iyengar hadn't come yesterday either. He'd complained of a bad stomach the day before. Granted he was rich, but who ate kaliyangudi halwa every day at his age? It must not have agreed with him.

Kaliyangudi halwa brought back sweet memories. That was a different time. His dead wife came to mind. *If only she were here*, his heart wept.

He sat down, leaning against a pillar. The goings-on at home were deepening his depression. Hunger squeezed at his stomach. The rasam rice and curd rice he'd had for lunch had long disappeared from his stomach. His daughter-in-law seemed to have deep-fried something, maybe crisp vadam or vathal, but nothing showed up on his lunch leaf. He bit his tongue to stop himself from asking her about it.

It had been 20 days since his son had lost his job. His poor daughter-in-law, what could she do? She had five mouths to feed, she seemed to be managing somehow.

The owner bhai at the clothes shop that his son worked at had asked him not to come back. He claimed that there had been some misappropriation. His son tried to explain in a hundred different ways that he had done no such thing, but bhai had been steadfast. He'd told him he could never enter the store again. When the old man went to beg him, he'd threatened to call the police, hadn't he?

Just last month, he'd seen his daughter-in-law go to Kathiresan's granddaughter's puberty function, wearing something dazzling around her neck and in her ears. He knew now that he was wrong to think it was some cheap gilt. If he asked her where she had got it from, she'd anyway bring the roof down with her crocodile tears.

The Iyengar's son was very influential. Iyengar had promised to talk to his son about a job and then he had disappeared for two days. The old man was growing utterly restless.

On top of it all, hunger was choking his stomach now. Back in the day, you'd get some puliyodharai, sweet pongal or white pongal as prasadam when you visited temples. These days, people offered the food to God and ran home with it instead of distributing it.

'Mama, you are Gopu's father, no?'

The old man squinted at the stranger. 'Who's this? I can't figure it out.' He didn't seem like a local.

'It's me, Agoram's son.'

'Which Agoram? Taluka office Agoram? Or cook Agoram?'

The stranger in front of him smiled lightly. 'I am cook Agoram's younger son Vaidyanathan. Gopu's classmate.'

'I heard you are all somewhere in America now?'

'Yes, my brother Swaminathan is also there only now. He studied with your older son Babu, remember?'

His heart compared the boys who'd studied with his sons for a moment. When wealth came, it brought with it beauty too, it seemed.

The old man nodded, asking, 'Your father passed away long back I remember... Your mother?'

'Amma was in Trichy with my Mama. She died 20 days ago. We've come here for her final rites. Her manjal kaani dowry land is here in Natham. We are thinking of disposing of it. How is Gopu? What is he up to now? It's been years since we met.'

That's right, the two brothers were thriving in America already, and as if that wasn't enough, they even had land to sell now for more cash. The old man burned with jealousy.

'Babu is in Nagpur. Gopu works here in the bhai's shop. He's the all-in-all there.'

'Very happy to hear this, Mama. Will you tell me if you know a good party I can sell the land to? It would be really convenient if I could get this done in the next 10 days.'

Hmm, wealth begets wealth, was that not the rule of the world? Wasn't land priced exorbitantly in that neighbourhood? *My son is suffering in a communal home.* The vexed old man thought of the Perumal he prayed to every day to calm himself.

'Who is farming these days? I hear all the land there is now being used to construct homes? Even our Gopu wanted to buy some land to build a home,' the old man said, lying for no reason.

'If it's for Gopu I will speak to my brother and sell the land at a lower rate. I don't even mind if he pays in instalments.'

'Why don't you give me your phone number? Gopu has gone with bhai to Surat. He will be back in four days,

I will ask him to call you then,' the old man said, sizing up the silhouette standing in front of him.

Suddenly, in the middle of these yarns he was spinning, the old man lost his sense of balance as he remembered the truth about his son. Bhai was already telling everyone that he had misappropriated funds. Mayavaram was a small town. What if someone told bhai that his son was buying land and building a house? He would be finished. The old man wet his dhoti a little in fear then.

Even as he searched his mind for words, he blurted out, 'Wait, wait, pa. I am saying the wrong thing here. My older son Babu is the one who told me he's looking for land in Nagpur, I seem to have mixed him up with Gopu. Gopu's kid is unwell and the treatment expenses are through the roof.' The old man said whatever he could to fix the situation and then wiped his face with the towel around his neck in relief. 'Okay, I will leave now. My son will come looking for me if I am late.'

The old man prepared to leave. He wondered if he should invite Vaidyanathan home as a courtesy but then decided against it right away.

A little disappointed, his son's friend said, 'Is that so, Mama? Okay, okay. I will take care of it.' The old man's ragged dhoti, torn here and there, stained everywhere, told him all he needed to know about his state.

He whipped out a wad of cash from his shirt pocket.

Wonder, oh wonder! How many notes. The old man hadn't seen that many ever in his life.

'Here,' Vaidyanathan said and held out a note. The old man couldn't tell if it was a 100- or 500-rupee note. They all looked the same now. He controlled the urge to take it and instead said, 'Maybe not as much as you, but both my sons earn too. They take good care of me.' He walked away, towards home, not looking back.

If he had 500 rupees, he could at least repay the provision store debt, the old man lamented as he walked, swaying this way and that.